Religion

Religion

A Theology for the Here and Now,
Volume Three

ANDY ROSS

RESOURCE *Publications* • Eugene, Oregon

RELIGION
A Theology for the Here and Now, Volume Three

Copyright © 2024 Andy Ross. All rights reserved. Except for brief quotations in critical publications or reviews, no part of this book may be reproduced in any manner without prior written permission from the publisher. Write: Permissions, Wipf and Stock Publishers, 199 W. 8th Ave., Suite 3, Eugene, OR 97401.

Resource Publications
An Imprint of Wipf and Stock Publishers
199 W. 8th Ave., Suite 3
Eugene, OR 97401

www.wipfandstock.com

PAPERBACK ISBN: 979-8-3852-2160-8
HARDCOVER ISBN: 979-8-3852-2161-5
EBOOK ISBN: 979-8-3852-2162-2

07/02/24

Scripture texts in this work are taken from the New American Bible, revised edition © 2010, 1991, 1986, 1970 Confraternity of Christian Doctrine, Washington, D.C. and are used by permission of the copyright owner. All Rights Reserved. No part of the New American Bible may be reproduced in any form without permission in writing from the copyright owner.

To Bill

Love is my religion.
—ZIGGY MARLEY

Contents

On Experience: A Prologue to Religion | 1

Spirituality | 6

Religious Thinking | 13

God(s) | 23

Religion Here and Now | 33

The Religious Process | 43

On Enlightenment: An Epilogue to Religion | 49

Bibliography | 55

On Experience
A Prologue to Religion

It is one thing merely to believe in a reality beyond the senses and another to have experience of it also.

—RUDOLPH OTTO[1]

WE EXIST BECAUSE OF God's single desire to know itself, and the phenomenon by which God knows and is known is experience. Creation is an expression of God. Each plant, animal, atom, and thought exists as a result of God's self-emptying (*kenosis*). As God pours itself into life, God-as-being becomes the multitude of forms that make up creation. And, as being is conscious, God-as-being is aware of all that God becomes. This awareness is the root of experience. As God is aware of life, so are we.

We know life because we experience life. Anything beyond the realm of experience could never be known. I know the warmth of the sun and the wetness of water because I have experienced them. I know love and grief, pleasure and pain, and the nuances of human emotion because I am having a human experience. As I experience life, the potentialities of my existence are actualized. These potentialities are unique to my circumstances, making my

---

1. Otto, *The Idea of the Holy*, 143.

lived experience invaluable to God. As I experience life, God's desire is fulfilled.

Each experience is unique because the specific configuration of forms that give rise to the experience can never and will never be repeated. God is aware of my life through the mechanisms of my human body and mind. I interact with the world around me—I see, touch, taste, hear, and smell. The forms with which I engage through these senses are unique to the moment. Sight, feeling, taste, sound, smell—each of these is made up of a vast array of forms rising and falling around me. As I am conscious of them, God is conscious of them through me.

I AM

As I touch these keys, God touches these keys. And, as I consider which keys to strike next, God considers. In the Gospel According to John, Jesus says, "Before Abraham came to be, I AM" (8:58).[2] This is both a reference to Exodus 3:14 and an insight into the nature of God. Our experience of life is grounded in God's experience of life within and through us. The feeling of finger touching key is grounded in the interaction of finger and key and the interpretation of the interaction by my mind. The root of the experience, however, is in God as consciousness.

I consider my unique self as the epicenter around which all of my lived experiences revolve. This assumption, however, is an illusion. My experiences are not grounded in my personhood. My personhood is merely another phenomenon which makes up the particularities of my experience. I experience life through my body and mind. Therefore, my body and mind are a part of the experience itself. As I touch these keys, I am experiencing both keys and fingers. As the experience is interpreted by my mind, I am experiencing the interpretation. I am not the forms rising within consciousness. I am consciousness.

---

2. All biblical quotes from the *New American Bible Revised Edition*.

God is experiencing my life. My unique self is the vehicle of that experience. At the center of who I am, there is a silent witness. This silent witness is the true self, the one who experiences all. As I let go of my attachment to the various ways that I define myself, I discover the one who is seeking to define. The joy of creation is the ongoing discovery of God through the experience of life. Each unique moment is the unfolding of God's desire. All forms are known by God as God experiences them in and through life.

WE ARE

The conception I have of myself and my life is both an illusion and a necessary step in the evolution of human experience. Existentially, we are all one. The Sanskrit term *namaste* can be translated as, "the place in me where we are one acknowledges the place in you where we are one." This greeting emphasizes the singularity of consciousness. The God that is experiencing my life is the God that is experiencing your life. God is eternally experiencing the innumerable forms that make up creation. What we consider our "personhood" is a specific subset of these forms.

I am a unique human being, meaning, I am a unique human expression of being itself. My mind draws all my ideas, memories, anxieties, etc. into a mosaic of personhood that we call the ego. The illusion of the self is the mind's continuous effort to create an individual out of the multiplicity of human experience. I am who I think I am. Similarly, as I interpret each experience within the backdrop of thought created by previous experiences, my perception of life evolves. Our understanding of life is rooted in the human experience. Everything we know about life is filtered through the lens of the human condition.

We are who we think we are, and life is what we think it is. These are limited human conceptions, yet it is their limitations that give them value. To know experientially is to bear witness to the uniqueness of the moment, to be conscious of it as God is. To know conceptually is to create a human image of the moment in the mind's eye. As humans, we seek to understand the particularities of each experience. Our minds weave a tapestry of thoughts together constructing a perspective unique to each of us.

CULTURE

As human beings, we share the human experience of life. This affords us a basis for understanding one another, as limited as this understanding may be. It is our ability to communicate that creates communal perspectives. Just as human beings share a common experience of life, those humans that form a cultural group share a unique way of understanding life. When you examine the culture within which you were raised, you notice certain modalities of being that just make sense. This is how we relate to one another and the world. This is how we conceptualize living. This is how we make meaning.

Cultures are in constant motion. With each new experience, our understanding of the world shifts. With each new interaction, we gain insight into the experience of another. Communication is essential to the evolution of culture. All I know is my experience of life until I bear witness to another's experience. Recent advancements in communication technology have increased the rate of cultural change. We are no longer communicating with one individual or group at a time. We are communicating with the world.

Religion is a specific subset of culture. The myriad ways that we experience God are catalogued within the world's religious traditions. Individual experiences of God give rise to spirituality. Communication makes the sharing of those experiences possible. And, as cultural groups form collective ways of engaging God, religions are born. Each religious tradition is influenced by the cultural and historical particularities of the environment within which it was born. As these particularities shift, so does the religion. Religion, like culture, is constantly evolving. And yet, there is something that sets religion apart.

THE TEXT

This text is a meditation on religion. It honors both the ongoing revelation of the reality that we call God and the unique ways that human beings have come to understand and engage that reality. I am not a historian or a textual critic, nor am I an expert on any specific religious tradition. This text does not claim absolute knowledge on the subject of religion, nor does it champion a single methodology when seeking to understand it. I am a theologian and a mystic, meaning that I discover the reality of God in the theological process. This text is a part of that process.

The religious traditions of the world fascinate and inspire me. The more I study the revelations of God, the more I feel God's presence. The religious landscape is a mosaic. Its various colors and patterns create a single image of the transcendent within and beyond the traditions. Frequently, I just sit back and witness the wonder of it all. Then again, I cannot help but entertain my innate curiosity.

Spirituality

> *The divine Ground of all existence is a spiritual Absolute, ineffable in terms of discursive thought, but (in certain circumstances) susceptible of being directly experienced and realized by the human being.*
>
> —Aldous Huxley[1]

God is the still center around which our lives revolve. This center is both the creative impulse for life and its silent witness. The eternal self is not the body or mind. These are merely vehicles of the human experience. The eternal self is the one who experiences all. We are both the movement of creation and its creator. And, just as we experience creation, we experience the one who creates.

BEAUTY AND LOVE

We are experiencing God always. As God is the being that becomes all things, we experience God within all things. And, as God is the consciousness that is aware of what God becomes, we experience God as consciousness. As we look out onto creation, we witness the beauty of forms rising and falling. We see the sun rise and a flower blossom. We feel the wind on our cheeks and the

---

1. Huxley, *The Perennial Philosophy*, 21.

grass beneath our feet. We hear the sound of music and the voices of our children. Creation is a vast web of interactions far beyond our comprehension, yet ever available to our senses.

God is the sun rising. Therefore, to witness the beauty of dawn is to witness the beauty of God. The beauty of the sunrise, however, is not found in the sunrise alone. Beauty is relational. The beauty of an object is discovered in the relationship between the object and the subject who beholds it. God is the sun and the one witnessing it rise. God witnessing God is beautiful. Embedded within each interaction is God's desire made manifest. When we discover beauty, we are peering into a mirror image of our deepest self.

Our experience of love is similar. Love in its myriad forms is God witnessing itself as other. Love often begins as a familiarity, a sense that the person or thing evoking that love is eternally "known." As one engages the object of love, the sensation deepens. The act of "falling in love" is the process by which one uncovers God's presence within the particularities of the relationship. The more vulnerable one is to the process, the deeper the decent into the unfathomable depths of God's presence.

God is present in all aspects of the lived experience. Therefore, the potential to find beauty and love in life is boundless. Yet there are certain places where beauty is undeniable. And there are certain people who make falling in love seem as natural as breathing. This is due to the wonder of our unique disposition as expressions of God's being. We are both united by our oneness and inimitable in our distinctness. To discover beauty and love in life is a gift. The manner by which we give and receive these gifts is our own.

MYSTERY

Just because we are experiencing God always does not mean that we are always aware of the experience. God's presence is hidden within the particularities of the moment. We experience life through a physical body, and the physical body only recognizes forms on the physical plane. Our senses are a part of the body. We see physical forms through physical eyes and so on and so forth. As extensions of energy, our bodies also register energetic shifts in the environment. We can literally feel the world change around us.

God is not a form rising within creation. God is not the energy moving within form.[2] God is the ineffable being within and beyond all form. We cannot see, taste, touch, smell, or hear God. We cannot feel when God moves. And our minds, which seek to conceptualize sensual experience, are not able to comprehend God's presence. Thoughts are subtle forms rising and falling on the mental plane. Thought forms, like all forms, are limited. God is unlimited. Our experience of God is the experience of being and consciousness. It is not tangible, but it is ever-present.

Beauty and love are words that describe a human experience of something beyond the senses. We can describe the way beauty makes us feel or how love affects our physical lives. We can conceptualize the environment wherein beauty is found, and we know the object of our love to be a physical expression just as we are. Yet there is a dimension to beauty and love that transcends physical reality. In fact, it is the very essence of beauty and love which lies beyond the veil of the senses.

The manifestations through which love and beauty are made known to us are tangible. The essence of love and beauty is not. It is the same with experiences of God. We understand the way that an encounter with the divine makes us feel. We can describe the circumstances surrounding the encounter. We may even be able to reconstruct the encounter. The core of the experience, however, remains a mystery. A being revealed through its creation, but never able to be fully grasped.

REVELATION

God is always revealing itself to us. This is not a choice on God's part, but an existential aspect of God's character. God is omnipresent—present within and beyond creation at all times and in all

---

2. In actuality, God is all things.

places.[3] Therefore, we have the capacity to experience God under any and all circumstances. In fact, we are experiencing God always; we are simply unaware of the experience—that is, until circumstances make God's presence undeniable.

You walk into a gothic cathedral and immediately feel a shift in the environment. The shift is physical and energetic. The physical forms within the space are arranged in a manner that set the space apart from the profane world.[4] Their arrangement causes the energy in the space to shift, allowing for a feeling of serenity. Yet the physical and energetic movement points toward an underlying reality. The more you linger in the space, the more you feel attuned to a still presence. It is within the space, and it is within you.

This is a spiritual experience—the root of spirituality. Whether the experience is facilitated by an environment or ritual designed to evoke it, or simply a serendipitous arrangement of trees on your morning walk, the nature of the interaction is the same. Spirituality is rooted in our experience of the transcendent within the imminent circumstances of our lives. We are typically engrossed in *maya*, a Sanskrit term used to describe the illusory nature of creation. We are physical beings caught up in a physical world. But the permanence of the world is an illusion.

Revelation is an unveiling of *maya*. During moments of revelation, we are keenly aware of a reality beyond that of the senses. We are able to see beyond sight and to hear beyond hearing. During spiritual experiences, we are transported through the profane circumstances of the moment into a still space within and beyond them. The environment of the senses is not lost on us, however. Instead, our experience of the environment is enlivened. The experience of the sacred enhances the experience of the profane. All things become harbingers of the one.

---

3. Recall that time and space are how we measure forms within creation; they are not aspects of God in itself.

4. Sacred and profane are terms often used to distinguish spaces of spiritual significance from ordinary spaces.

Sacred Spaces

Any moment can facilitate an encounter with the divine. Yet there are certain moments where the encounter is more likely. For instance, there are many who find God in nature. All of creation pulses with the presence of the divine, but the natural world radiates it. If God is life, then it would seem natural to find God in places where life flows naturally and abundantly. It is not that God is absent from the city or supermarket. In reality, there is no distinction between the sacred and profane. Some spaces are just less distracting.

Nature is created by the serendipitous flow of life. The scaredness of nature lies within its ability to evoke an experience of the one life moving through the many. Human-created spaces are designed for a multitude of purposes—economical, practical, social, etc. For instance, economical spaces are meant to draw your attention to commerce. They are designed to seduce the participant into a frenzy of material desire. God is fully present in the billboards of Time Square. We are simply too distracted to notice.

Human-created sacred spaces are designed to facilitate an encounter with the divine. Instead of distracting the participant from the stillness within and beyond the circumstantial, the space pulls the attention toward it. Every element within a sacred space points to God. The sacred nature of the space is shaped by the intention of those who are responsible for its construction. One must experience the divine in order to facilitate that experience for others. Spirituality begets spirituality.

Sacred objects

The creation of sacred objects (art, texts, iconography, etc.) follows the same pattern as the creation of sacred spaces. The one creating the object has a specific experience of the divine. The experience is shaped by the particularities of the moment. History, culture, temperament—these all play a role in how the experience is understood. Recall that the experience of God cannot be qualified. Therefore, the individual or group must rely upon the tools available to them in order to create a representation of their limited understanding. The artist renders, the builder builds, the writer writes, but they all do so as an expression of their spiritual experience.

According to Catholic theologian Karl Rahner, what we call "grace" is God's constant self-communication.[5] God is eternally communicating with us through creation. As a part of creation, we participate in that communication. It is our capacity for self-awareness that creates what theologians call special revelation. Special revelation is the result of human engagement with the divine and is, therefore, able to speak directly to the human condition.

I am having an experience of God, i.e., God is being revealed to me through the circumstances of the moment. My talent in a specific area of human expression affords me the opportunity to communicate this revelation in a special way. If what I create is able to facilitate an experience of the divine in others, I have succeeded in rendering a special revelation. Religion is sustained by those who are able to participate in the ongoing revelation of God. As the human condition changes, so does the nature of special revelation.

Our experience of God is the root of spirituality. Whether we stumble upon it or seek it out, this experience has the potential to change the course of our lives. God is the ground of being—the root of all existence, including our own. Therefore, to experience God is to experience the place within and beyond ourselves that cannot be altered by the trials and tribulations of life. To discover the divine is to discover an inexhaustible source of peace, love, and joy. The experience, however, is only the beginning.

DISCIPLINE

During moments of revelation, we are able to recognize the presence of God within and beyond the circumstances of our lives.

---

5. See Karl Rahner's *Foundations of Christian Faith*.

We catch a glimpse of an underlying reality seemingly more real than the one we are accustomed to. Yet waiting for God to appear in random encounters is not enough to create a foundation for religion. Spirituality is more than the experience of God. It is our dedication to recreate and deepen the experience.

Most human beings have stumbled upon a divine encounter at some point in their lives. They may not call the encounter "divine"; they may not reflect on the encounter much at all. But for those who are curious, the moment is enough to draw them into a spiritual discipline. The spiritual experience is God made known through the circumstances of the moment. The discipline is the practice of recreating and deepening the experience.

You follow a path in the woods to a small clearing. The boundaries of this clearing are trees on three sides, a brook on the fourth, the ground beneath your feet, and the sky above you. Existentially, this space is no different from any other. The particulars of the space are unique due to the unique configuration of forms, but this is true for all spaces. And yet, this particular configuration of forms evokes a sense of connected stillness, a feeling that there is something within and beyond the elements.

Your experience in this small clearing is enough to draw you back. You return to the place in the woods in order to recreate the experience. Perhaps you are successful; perhaps you are not. Yet, if you are determined, the stillness will find you again. It is the determination to recreate divine encounters that is the bedrock of religion. The more we return to the source of the encounter, the more likely we are to recreate it. As we do so, the environment shifts. The more we look for God, the more we find God.

Religious Thinking

> *The religions begin by assuring us that if we could see the full picture we would find it more integrated than we normally suppose.*
>
> —HUSTON SMITH[1]

A SINGLE EXPERIENCE OF the divine has the potential to alter the course of our lives. Though we are accustomed to viewing creation as a series of physical encounters, this perspective is the result of human conditioning. We accept our human understanding of the world because this is all that we know. We feel with a human body and think with a human brain. Spiritual experiences disrupt linear thinking by opening the body and mind to a reality beyond the realm of the senses. One glimpse into the eternal and the human being is never the same.

TRANSCENDENCE

We develop our understanding of reality through our experience of reality. We are taught the meaning of this experience by those who have come before us, and we experiment with meaning through our day-to-day encounters. Our perspective is constantly shifting. My understanding of the world is not the same today as it

---

1. Smith, *The World's Religions*, 388.

was yesterday. Reality is what we think it is. The mind is a part of creation and is, therefore, able to process sensual experience and add to its storehouse of knowledge—knowledge increases and our understanding of reality expands.

Spiritual experiences are both sensual and not. We are a part of creation and, therefore, experience God through creation. Creation, however, is not the root of the spiritual encounter. When we experience God, we are drawn into a presence within and beyond the realm of the senses. God is here, deep within the fabric of the forms surrounding me. And God is beyond them. The "within and beyond" of the spiritual experience is the foundation of religious thinking. The term typically used to the describe this mode of thinking is "transcendence."

Within

The "within" of transcendence is the presence of God within all things. We are expressions of God's being and, therefore, experience God within the deepest caverns of the self. God is closer to us than our breathing. We are walking expressions of the divine, lost to its presence due to the constant distraction of body and mind. I feel the beat of my heart and the ache of my bones. I am bombarded by emotion and thought. And, then, I am quiet. I settle into the moment and find that there is a peace within me. This peace is untouchable and unfathomable. It just is.

Divine encounters awaken the still voice of God within us. The peace that we feel is the eternal state of the divine. It is not a product of our lived experience; it is the foundation of it. All spiritual experiences resonate from within. For humans, life begins and ends with the body. Our experience of God, therefore, is embodied. Even as we experience God in the other, we experience God within. God is looking out. And God is looking back.

As God is the being that becomes all things, God is experienced within all things. The God that is within us recognizes the God that is within the forms surrounding us. Just as I discover the peace of God within me, I discover the peace of God within creation. I find God in nature and my family; I find God in the temple and synagogue; I find God in warmth and in darkness. The experience of God is one—a single presence within all things. This presence cannot be grasped by the body or mind. It is transcendent. And, as transcendent, it is also beyond.

Beyond

The term panentheism refers to the understanding that God is within all things, yet all things do not encompass what God is. God is not simply "in here"; God is "out there." God is beyond all forms—the forest, ocean, planet, and universe. It is not that God is larger than creation. Size does not apply to God. God is omnipresent, within and beyond all things at all times. The "beyond" of transcendence is God's presence as that which extends beyond the boundaries of form.

Just as God is experienced in the depths of the person, God is experienced as a boundless, unreachable horizon. We are not simply guided by a voice within, we are pulled by a voice beyond. The universe, though incomprehensible in its vastness, is a created thing. And, like all created things, the universe has boundaries. Space is not infinite—no form is infinite. The beyond of transcendence is not God's immeasurability. It is God's formlessness. God is the one reaching, and the one who is forever beyond reach.

"Religious thinking" refers to the effect that spiritual experiences have on perception and perspective. The experience of God opens the individual to a transcendent reality. Once the individual is aware of this reality, the perspective shifts in order to accommodate it. The result is a mode of thought which utilizes sense perception to qualify the unqualifiable. The paradox of religious thinking is the tension between the unknown and the desire to know. This tension creates a unique disposition in the human that is often misunderstood.

FAITH

All that we know of reality is our experience of it. We experience forms rising and falling around us and within us. Our experience of these forms creates sense perceptions in the mind which contribute to a mosaic of thoughts that we call perspective. Each experience changes the way we view creation. Our experience of the divine is no exception. We encounter the divine through creation and form images in our mind based upon the particularities of the moment. It is the source of the encounter that is unqualifiable. And it is the source that religious thoughts are seeking to qualify.

By definition, a transcendent reality can never be known. Thus the term transcendence is only meaningful as a paradox. I accept that there is something beyond what I can sense. I accept that there is something beyond what I can know. I accept it because I experience it. The closer I look, the less of it I see. I farther I reach, the less of it I feel. The more I try and wrap my mind around it, the more it eludes me. And yet, it is always here. I cannot explain how I know this. I just do.

Faith is often equated with belief. This is because religious belief is a mental expression of religious faith. However, while religious belief is the summation of thoughts regarding what the transcendent is understood to be, faith is the disposition of one's entire self in relation to the transcendent. We believe because we have faith. And yet, a belief system can never fully encapsulate the experience of faith. Experience precedes understanding, and a thought should never be misconstrued as the experience itself.[2]

Because I am eternally experiencing God, I have eternal access to God's presence. Though this presence transcends my ability to comprehend it, I am a part of it and it is a part of me. Once I recognize this experience, I can choose to engage it. I can reorient my life around the presence of God and act in a manner that deepens my relationship with it. This reorientation is the foundation of faith. I turn toward the divine in thought, word, and deed. I accept

---

2. We experience thoughts just as we experience creation. In reality, the two cannot be separated.

that I will never grasp what I have found, or what has found me, but I accept it all the same. And when I accept the presence of God, I find it everywhere.

RELIGIOUS THOUGHT

Religious thought has evolved into such a wide array of images, categories, and institutions that it is hard to believe that it all stems from a single source. Yet all one has to do is embrace the breadth of human perspective to understand the breadth of religious thought. Perspective is the summation of a human's thoughts about creation. These thoughts are the product of experience. As no two humans share the same set of experiences, no two humans share the same perspective. We are all experiencing the same reality. We simply view it from different lenses.

God is one, a single divine reality within and beyond all things. Each and every experience of God, whether facilitated by a shaman or Bob Marley song, is an experience of this one reality understood in a variety of ways. These varieties[3] depend upon the perspective of the individual and the unique circumstances surrounding the experience. In the Torah, God says, "Let us make human beings in our image, after our likeness" (Genesis 1:26). This verse describes the human being as an expression of God, bearing its likeness. It would, however, be equally true to state that we create God in our image.

Personification

Our perspective is human. We view creation through human eyes and understand it with a human brain. It is, therefore, natural that we personify everything. We see human faces in the clouds, create human stories about the plant and animal world, and give names and personalities to inanimate objects. This behavior is a conscious and unconscious way to form relationships with the world around

---

3. A reference to *The Varieties of Religious Experience* by William James.

us. As human beings, we naturally relate to other humans. No matter how difficult it may seem to walk a mile in another human's shoes, we are built for it.

Every human being is different. And yet, we are all human. We come into life with a similar set of tools and move through life with similar needs and desires. Try as we might, we will never know what it is to be a cat or a sycamore. This does not, however, stop us from trying. Personification, or anthropomorphism, is grounded in an effort to create relationships. And relationships, like love, are built upon our existential relation to all things. I may not know what it is to be a sycamore, but, like a sycamore, I am an expression of God's being.

The human experience of God is not existentially unique. All of creation is experiencing God as God is experiencing all of creation. It is our capacity for self-reflection that creates human images of God. Just as we personify creation, we personify God. As we reflect on the experience of God, our minds create images in order to qualify the experience. These images are shaped by the circumstances of the encounter in relation to previous experiences. The result is a category of thinking that is specific to the divine, but nevertheless human.

Imago Dei

Every understanding of God is a human understanding, and every image of God is a human image. Even seemingly non-personified expressions, such as the *Tao*, are grounded in the human relationship to the divine. These images serve as a means of creating a conscious relationship with the ground of being. And in so doing, we are able to direct our thoughts, words, and actions towards God itself. Religious thought is not necessary in order to relate to God—we are always relating to God. It is, however, necessary in order to participate consciously in that relationship.

Homosapien means discerning human. Our species is defined by many characteristics, but none is more prominent than our capacity for acquiring knowledge. This is what makes us a unique species among those that we have encountered thus far. Human beings have created entire universes within the mind. We have pulled from our experience of creation and fashioned great storehouses of meaning and understanding. Spirituality begins with the experience of God. Religion begins in the mind.

Most adherents of a religious tradition can claim, in some manner, that they "know God." This statement is accurate if you understand what it means "to know." To know something is to experience it firsthand and then to create a mental representation of that something in order to place the experience within the context of the larger experience of creation. All who experience God can come to know God if they choose to do so. In fact, there is an entire branch of study concerned with the knowledge of God.

THEOLOGY

St. Anslem of Canterbury defines theology as "faith seeking understanding." This definition is important because it highlights a central component of the religious process. A human being experiences God (spirituality). She then orients her life toward the deepening of that experience (faith). During this process, she creates images in her mind qualifying the source of the experience in relation to her overall experience of creation (theology). Each human being exists within a greater context of spiritual experience and imagination and, therefore, contributes to its myths and rituals (religion).

Though it is true that many do not spend their time in theological contemplation, none can escape the mind's incessant drive for knowledge. The tension between the experience of God and the ineffable nature of the experience is such that the mind can never be satisfied. The experience itself, along with the disposition of faith, informs us that we are experiencing something. It is this "something" that pulls us into relationship. The deeper the relationship, the more we experience the peace, love, and joy of God's being.

As long as we are able to accept the disparity between experience and knowledge, the theological process continues. And because the mind cannot grasp the divine, theological images continue to evolve. Each subsequent set of images captures a unique aspect of the experience, creating an ever-expanding encyclopedia of theological expression. There is, however, an inevitable shadow side to this human condition. When the human is not able to sit in the tension of not-knowing, the icon becomes an idol.

Iconography and Idolatry

An icon is a religious image which serves to reference the object of the spiritual experience. Whether an idea, image, or text, icons are not objects of worship, but objects through which the divine is consciously engaged. If religious thoughts are mental images which seek to qualify experiences of the divine, icons are images (both mental and physical) which serve as facilitators of future experiences. Not all religious thought becomes iconography, just as not all spiritual anecdotes become mythology. Icons must have transformative power.

The mind is constantly creating images in reference to human experience. And though these images can never truly convey the actuality of the experience, creation offers reference points to solidify the images. A healthy mind will compare the images it holds for reality with the experience of reality itself. I walk out into the world, and the images I maintain for the world are regulated through comparison with previous experience. It is impossible, however, for the mind to find a reference point for the images it creates for the spiritual experience. During spiritual encounters the mind works to penetrate their source, but in vain.

Thus we return to the tension which facilitates the theological process and the development of iconography. The litmus test for the accuracy of religious thought is not its factual resemblance to the source of religious experience. A factual resemblance is not possible. The test, instead, is the thought's ability to recreate the experience. When I consider God, do I experience God? When

I reflect on the source of my spirituality, do I feel connected with that source? Religious thoughts must always be on the verge of becoming iconography. Otherwise, they will inevitably become idolatrous.

The inevitable danger of religious thinking is the mind's need to qualify the source of the religious encounter. Because it is difficult to exist within the tension of theological speculation, oftentimes the mind will identify an image as the source itself. Once an image is identified with God, the transformative power diminishes and the icon becomes an idol. Unlike an icon, an idol is worshiped as a divine object, instead of an object through which the divine is addressed. These objects not only obstruct the deepening of spiritual experience, they become a catalyst for religious violence.

IMMANENCE

The function of iconography, as an extension of religious thinking, is to create an immanent relationship with a transcendent reality. As transcendent, God is within and beyond all things at all times. Although we are experiencing God always, we cannot comprehend God as the object of our experience. It is not that God is too far removed from creation. In actuality, God is closer to us that our thoughts. It is simply that God is not an object at all. Instead, God is the being which gives rise to objects (forms). It would be folly, however, to assume that God cannot be experienced as immanent.

We experience God within and through creation. God after all is the being that becomes all things. As we consider God as the source of the religious experience, whether or not we use the term God, our minds create images in reference to it. If these images are successful in helping to recreate the experience, we have successfully created an immanent expression of a transcendent reality. Of course, the immanent expression, like all expressions, bears the likeness of God. God is all things and all things are God. The function of religious thought and, therefore iconography, is not to bring God closer. The function of religious thought is revelation.

The religious landscape boasts countless expressions of the divine—Gods and Goddesses, Buddhas and Bodhisattvas, *Tao* and emptiness. Each is grounded in the experience of God, and each is an expression of the evolution of religious thought. They are one and they are many. There is opportunity for us all to discover the transcendent within the caverns of religious expression. And if we cannot find it, all we have to do is consider our own experience. Then, perhaps, we will find our own deity.

God(s)

It would not be too much to say that myth is the secret opening through which the inexhaustible energies of the cosmos pour into human cultural manifestation.

—JOSEPH CAMPBELL[1]

WE ORGANIZE AND GIVE meaning to our experience of creation within the mind. As we experience life, our thoughts evolve and new meanings are created. Communication provides us the opportunity to share ideas, providing a bedrock for cultural evolution. Our experience of the divine shapes religious thought and provides images of the transcendent that are sometimes able to facilitate similar experiences. As these images gain momentum, iconography is integrated into the evolving cultural landscape, and the religious process continues.

WARNING

It would be impossible to outline the full spectrum of religious evolution. As we examine the history of religious expression, certain patterns emerge, but even these patterns are intrinsic to the religious process. My understanding of iconography, mythology, and religious ritual cannot be separated from my experience of

1. Campbell, *The Hero with a Thousand Faces*, 3.

the divine within and through these phenomena. Conversely, the desire to be academically objective often ignores the very experience that gives rise to religion in the first place. There is benefit in both the academic pursuit and the phenomenological, but neither can grasp the breadth of religiosity in the world.

My understanding of the evolution of religious expression is limited to my experience as a mystic and theologian. The outline presented in this chapter has been influenced by religious scholarship, but even the most objective attempt to define religion falls upon the ears of one who finds God everywhere. I am not bothered by my lack of objectivity. It is not the purpose of this text to provide an objective account of religious evolution. Instead, I hope to examine the history of religious expression from a wide and personal angle. The following is not for you to agree or disagree with. It is merely a path from then to now.

CONNECT BACK

Early expressions of religious thought are difficult to comprehend. Religiosity is so integrated into our modern understanding of the world that it would be impossible to separate our current views of creation from the religious expressions that support or oppose them. Even the militant atheists in their opposition to religious thought have conversely been shaped by it. And yet, all current religious traditions have within them the seeds of their most ancient brethren. From the vantage point of a single belief system, you can see back to the beginning.

Though the modern spiritual experience is understood through the lens of modernity, it is the same experience as it has always been. The transcendent is changeless. Thus we are experiencing the same transcendent reality as our ancestors. Though the origins of the word religion are uncertain, one possible meaning is "to connect back." The connection that religion facilitates is twofold. On the one hand, religion connects us to the foundation of life. The religious process takes us back to the beginning—to the origin of life itself. It returns us to the one that becomes the many.

God(s)

On the other hand, religion connects us to those who have come before us. The currents of religiosity are alive in the modern human. This is of course the reality of all cultural phenomena. The human condition is built from the ground up. We exist as the result of all who have come before us. Our patterns of thought contain within them the self-conscious musings of the first homo sapiens.[2] The current religious landscape is both complex and integrated. Each religious tradition is both culturally and historically unique and contains within it the original seeds of religious thought.

ANIMISM

The earliest spiritual experiences led humans to consider the relationship between the reality of the senses and the reality beyond. Their experience of the transcendent was not yet organized into a theological system. We take for granted our theological and philosophical ancestry. Our distant relatives had no such foundation. They did, however, have the experience itself—a transcendent reality within and beyond all things. And this experience was enough to forge an understanding of the spiritual world that would become the bedrock of religion.

The development of reflective consciousness was not instantaneous. Instead, our ancestors became reflectively aware of their surroundings and themselves in subtle degrees. We could, therefore, postulate that early experiences of the divine were held with the same sense of wonder as experiences of the physical world. We are experiencing the spiritual, energetic, and physical planes continuously and simultaneously. Modern humans have developed an understanding of creation that subverts the spiritual realm to the physical. Early humans, on the other hand, experienced all of life as enigmatic.

There is the world that I can taste, touch, smell, see, and hear. Then there is a world within and beyond the senses. Our ancestors experienced both as essential to their wellbeing. The physical

---

2. In truth, we contain within us the evolutionary footprints of all living things.

world provided sustenance in the form of food and shelter. But what of the spiritual realm? What of the realm within and beyond the world that they inhabited? According to early religious thought, the spiritual realm was causally linked to the physical. Just as we are sustained by the bounty that is all around us, all of life is sustained by the divine—one reality animating another.

Animism has been expressed in various forms throughout ancient history, but the basic structure of thought is the same. There is a transcendent reality that animates this one. The nature of that reality and how it would come to be organized continue to evolve. For our purposes, we only need to understand the importance of animism as the basis for all religious thought. All religious traditions posit the existence of a transcendent reality within and beyond this one. Once human beings became reflectively aware of the spiritual experience, an animistic worldview was inevitable.

Shaman

The scientific revolution has provided countless advancements and innovations, but it has also contributed to a culture where what can be measured is prioritized over what cannot. Early humans had yet to develop this materialistic approach to the physical world. This does not mean, however, that our ancestors had privileged access to the divine. Their experience of the physical, energetic, and spiritual planes was akin to ours. It is their understanding of these planes that differed. Our ancestors required guidance just as we do.

There will always be those who have an intrinsic understanding of the spiritual realm. This does not mean that some have more access to it than others. Recall that we are all experiencing the fullness of God's presence at all times. This presence cannot be divided or measured out in degrees. Some, however, seem to recognize the reality within and beyond ours in a transformative way. This was true for our ancestors just as it is true for us today. The early shamans[3] were humans that recognized the value of communing with the world within and beyond ours. And they developed practical ways to do so.

Though it is impossible to know the spiritual practices of the first humans, there is an overall template developed by the early shamans that carries over today. If there is a transcendent reality that animates the physical one, then it was the role of the shaman to commune with that reality. In certain meditative or "trance" states, the shaman would journey into the world of the spirit in order to better understand how the tribe could maintain harmony and balance between the realms. The shaman's ability to navigate these realities gave him/her a privileged place within the community. Spiritual leaders have always granted insight into the divine, helping others to find peace.

KAMI

The early shamans created the prototypes for interacting consciously with the spiritual realm. The integration of these practices into tribal life formed a consensus among the community regarding the relationship between realms. Our understanding of life evolves as our experiences do. Thus, as spiritual practices became a common experience of tribal life, the understanding of spirit began to evolve. The next step in this evolution was the development of elemental spirits or *kami*.

Kami is a term used in the Shinto traditions of Japan. It refers to deities or spirits in general but, more specifically, as the governing force behind natural phenomena. The shamans created spiritual practices that allowed tribal members to participate in the animating reality within and beyond the physical world. As they did so, members of the community, under the guise of the shaman, began to create mental images of the transcendent. Perhaps the animating force behind the forest is a forest spirit or *kami*. This

---

3. Shaman in this text is used as a generic term for ancient spiritual leader. The term typically applies to specific spiritual leaders within certain indigenous cultures.

spirit would have a personal relationship with the trees and plants. Thus, for the first time, humans created personified versions of the spiritual realm.

Creation is both vast and mysterious. The primary function of the reflective mind is to create stability out of a chaotic environment. The spiritual experience creates a feeling of peace within the chaos. Therefore, it is natural to seek stability in our relationship with the transcendent. Our relationship with the divine is constant. To create meaning, however, we must personify that relationship. *Kami* were forces with which we could commune. Each element within the environment had a related *kami*. And understanding the *kami* was integral to understanding creation itself.

If all of creation is animated by the divine, it is a natural next step to qualify the nature of the relationship. Thus the animating spirits began to take on the characteristics of the natural elements that they supported. The *kami* of the wood was dark and mysterious, the *kami* of the sun was benevolent and powerful, and the *kami* of rain was nurturing yet precarious.[4] By understanding the nature of the *kami*, our ancestors could understand the nature of creation. And more importantly, they could participate in rituals that would serve the creative spirits.

Myth and Ritual

Kami were a major development in religious thinking. As humans began to personify the transcendent elements within and beyond creation, a whole system of myth and ritual inevitably followed. Human beings are story tellers. As we ascribe meaning to our experience of life, there develops a natural correlation between understanding and narrative. Our understanding of the world comes in the form of truth claims about the state of reality. This is what I believe is happening to me and around me. To communicate this understanding, we contextualize the truth in narrative. This is the story of my life.

4. These are generalizations and may not reflect the actual beliefs of ancient communities.

GOD(S)

Mythology can be defined as a narrative representation of the transcendent realm in relation to the physical. If we believe that *kami* behave as we behave, which is a natural result of personification, then they too have a story. As our ancestors communed with the *kami*, they developed a narrative understanding of the *kami's* existence. And these narratives evolved as the communities did. Stories were told and retold and, more importantly, ritualized. A mythic understanding of the transcendent is not actualized until it is participated in through ritual.

Humans develop a narrative understanding of the transcendent so that they may consciously participate in the creative process. Stories are enacted through ritual so that the community may discover that they exist in relation to "the other." The relationship between the transcendent and immanent is ongoing and ever present. Mythology is a symbolic representation of an ineffable reality. This reality, being the backdrop of all created things, is not merely imagined. Ritual is a conscious reminder of the true nature of creation.

The mythologizing of the *kami* was a major steppingstone in the evolution of religious expression. Myth and ritual gave humans an opportunity to find themselves in the narrative of creation. We could commune with the spirits of nature. We could express our gratitude for an abundant season and ask for aid during turbulent times. In essence, the story of our lives grew larger and more inclusive. We had discovered a way to find peace and meaning in the mysterious darkness of the spiritual realm. Its story was our story, and we could participate in it.

GODS

Creation is not stagnant, and neither are the narratives of those who participate in creation. As our experience of life expands, so does our understanding. And, as our understanding evolves, so do the narratives that express that understanding. The story of the *kami* had to evolve. The groups who ritualized those stories were changing rapidly. Simple tribal structures were growing into complex communities with governing hierarchies. Thus it was only natural that the spirits would develop their own hierarchy.

The personification of the transcendent encompasses all elements of the human condition. Our fears and anxieties, hopes and dreams, art and social structures—all play a role in the images created for those who occupy the spiritual realm.[5] Communities would create unique spiritual hierarchies based upon their own institutions and traditions. A well-known example of an ancient spiritual hierarchy is Egypt in the time of the pharaohs.

The gods and goddesses of ancient Egypt reflected the power of natural elements along with the created impulses of the community. *Ra*, the god of the sun, was the most powerful deity in the Egyptian pantheon. Like the sun, he had the power to give life and presided over the other gods as the sun presides over the earth. *Ra* had many forms, but his most prevalent was that of a large man with the head of a falcon. The other gods were personified in a similar fashion, each taking on the characteristics of the element or elements they governed.

The spiritual hierarchies of ancient civilizations differ based upon the lives and structures of those societies. The existential relationship between gods and society, however, remains the same. The nature of the gods reflects the nature of the community that worships them. As a community evolves, so do the deities of that community. The spiritual plane is changeless—it is the constant ineffable backdrop of creation. Our understanding of the spiritual plane, however, continues to expand, allowing for a more inclusive view of the transcendent. With each step in our religious evolution, we gain more insight into the world within and beyond.

GOD

The majority of the religious traditions thriving in the world today have developed a monotheistic or monistic understanding of the transcendent. By the time Jesus of Nazareth was born, Judaism had

---

5. Recall that the spiritual realm is one, but we conceptualize it utilizing a plethora of images.

accepted *Yahweh* as the one true God. This notion that there was a single deity governing the cosmos carried over into Christianity and Islam. And though the Hindu traditions espouse thousands of gods and goddesses, most Hindus believe that these are all manifestations of *Brahman*, the one supreme reality.

Monotheism should not be viewed as a higher form of religious expression than polytheism. One is not more or less true than the other. The truth of religion is in its ability to facilitate an authentic experience of the transcendent. The rise of monotheism and, subsequently, monism, was a reflection of the spiritual lives of the human community. Developments in religious and philosophical thinking during the axial age[6] began to posit the existence of a single divine reality.

The non-personified *Tao* of Lao Tzu and the personified father figure of *Yahweh* can seem at the outset to be opposing views of the transcendent. While, like all religious traditions, they are culturally and historically unique, they share the belief that the creator is one. The primary difference in the monistic view of Taoism and the monotheistic view of Judaism is the emphasis that they place on God's oneness. Monistic religions emphasize the oneness of God—its characteristic as a single unified reality. Monotheistic religions, on the other hand, focus on the belief that there is one God as opposed to many.

vs. Science

The belief that God is one has been the prominent view in the world's religious traditions during the common era. Though the variants of belief are so expansive that many cannot recognize the seeds of one in the other, the currents of monotheism and monism are strong. And while some would argue that the scientific revolution has debunked religious views, it has actually contributed to the rise of new religious expressions, both conservative and progressive.

---

6. The period just before the Common Era when the ideas emerged that would shape all subsequent modern philosophy and theology.

The enlightenment ushered in a new reality of scientific investigation and achievement. Advancements in scientific thought over the last few centuries have changed the way we view creation. Religious responses, in general, have been two-fold. On the one hand, certain religious groups have embraced the new paradigm. These groups have widened their understanding of God's relationship to the environment, taking on an ecologically minded theology, and they have utilized advancements in historical criticism to better understand sacred texts.

On the other hand, there have been those who have adopted a more conservative religious view in direct opposition to scientific achievements. For example, many Christian fundamentalists accept the Bible as the inerrant word of God, literally true and free from human error. There are those who believe that the gap between science and religion is widening, with no resolution in site. The gap, however, is an illusion created by those who refuse to see the need for both. The resolution is not only simple, it is inevitable.

Religious thought is the natural result of the human condition. Since the earliest developments within the self-reflective mind, humans have been musing over their experience of the transcendent. Religion proper is the way we organize these musings into participatory systems of myth and ritual. Because the development of religious thought is tied to the development of the human perspective in general, as humans evolves, so do their religions. We cannot consciously guide this evolution, no matter how much we would like to. All we can do is contribute to it. We can, however, consider what is to come.

Religion Here and Now

> *A modern theology must look unflinchingly into the heart of a great darkness and be prepared, perhaps, to enter into the cloud of unknowing.*
>
> —KAREN ARMSTRONG[1]

EACH NEW EXPERIENCE BRINGS with it the possibility of a shift in perspective. Human beings experience the transcendent within and through creation. Therefore, as humans are changed by their experience of creation, their understanding of the transcendent changes as well. New perspectives facilitate new understandings which, in turn, create wider views of reality. The more of reality that the human is able to grasp, the more of God. It is not that God grows or changes. On the contrary, God is the changeless that gives rise to change. We are the ones who change. And we are the ones who, in turn, create new traditions.

THE COMMUNICATION REVOLUTION

Communication is the foundation of culture. It is our ability to communicate with each other that makes the transmission of experience possible. All I know of creation is my experience of it

---

1. Armstrong, *The Case for God*, 278.

until someone chooses to share their experience with me.[2] The sharing of information creates the collective "we." Culture is the legacy of collective experience. It is an expression of our experience of life as it is transmitted via art, music, science, etc. This legacy makes it possible for the human perspective to expand. Experiences are cataloged and passed down from generation to generation, with each new generation standing on the shoulders of their predecessors.

Over the history of our species, methods of communication have evolved. With each new method (language, writing, telephone, internet, etc.) our ability to share information increases. Recently, we have entered a new phase in the evolution of communication. The global availability of high-speed internet has made the mass transmission and consumption of information, not only possible, but inevitable. There is a vast library of information at our fingertips. If there is something that we are interested in, all we have to do is "search" it. We have become the recipients of instantaneous world culture.

Positive

Information is a precious resource. The more information that a society has available to it, the greater its potential for growth. This is due to the nature of information, regardless of type or viability. Information is synthesized reflections on human experience. Each word, paragraph, opinion, and research product is an expression of the thought processes of individuals and communities. When we gather information, we are afforded access to the lives of others. The more information at our fingertips, the more lives we can know, and the more perspectives we can entertain.

---

2. When someone communicates with me, I am still limited to my experience of the information that is communicated.

Negative

For the majority of our history, we have assimilated information slowly. This is due, in large part, to its availability. We can communicate with others and learn as much about their lives as we are willing to hear. We can read the stories and findings of the world's authors, scientists, and historians. And we can listen to the conversations that are happening around us—personal, official, televised, etc. The internet, however, has provided us with high-speed information in the form of easily digestible data bits. In fact, this new wave of information has been designed for just that—ease of access. Each internet page is vying for our attention and working tirelessly to obtain it.

Advancements in communication, like all advancements, come with a price. Not only do these advancements require infrastructure to make them globally viable, they require a shift in the human psyche. The more information available to the human being, the more imperative the ability to discern truth. Since the dawn of self-reflection, we have measured the accuracy of information against our experience of life. Information gathered from sources, be they known or unknown, is placed within the context of our experiential understanding. Either the information resonates with my experience of life or it does not. Even information that challenges my known experience must resonate with the overall structure of my psyche.

TRUTH

We are having a subjective experience of an objective reality. Truth is the place where subjectivity and objectivity meet. What is often understood by "truth" (material truth) is reality in actuality. What is actually happening in the world around me? What is actually happening in the world within me? Then we have conceptual truth, such as the truth of goodness and beauty. What is good and how do I know? What is beauty and how do I know? Finally, we have theological truth. What is God? These may seem like distinct areas of concern, but, in actuality, they are only different in degree.

Material Truth

Truth in its most comprehensible form concerns measurable phenomena—what we can know about physical reality. We experience creation through the senses. We are physical expressions of being having a physical experience of life. In terms of the physical world, truth is measured by our mind's ability to match and comprehend reality's physical elements. The role of the physical sciences is to create tools that deepen our collective awareness of physical reality. Due to our subjective experience, we are limited in our capacity to know life. But together we can come close.

Conceptual Truth

All truth is technically conceptual, meaning all truth is based upon the relationship between concepts and reality. Conceptual truth as a specific degree of truth is limited to concepts regarding subtle phenomena. Beauty, for example, is not measurable. We experience certain measurable elements as beautiful, but beauty in itself is relational. When I discern something or someone as beautiful, I am reflecting on my relationship to it. When I behold this thing, I behold it as beautiful—meaning, this is how I conceptualize my experience of it.

Similarly, when we speak of goodness, we are describing our orientation toward thoughts, words, and actions that we consider "good." Thus goodness does not exist as a measurable phenomenon. Goodness is the conceptualization of our orientation toward actions that we deem as ultimately beneficial to life. Do beauty and goodness exist? Yes, they exist because we experience them individually and collectively. The truth of their existence, however, cannot be measured. We must discover conceptual truth within ourselves and society.

Theological Truth

Theological truth concerns the truth of God—whether God exists and what can or cannot be known about it. We are experiencing God always, just as we are experiencing creation, beauty, and goodness. Thus truth in every degree is the relationship between our subjective experience of phenomena and the phenomena themselves. Our experiential relationship with God is similar to our experiential relationship with the material world, meaning we are having a subjective experience of an objective reality. We can know nothing of this reality beyond our experience. This knowledge, this truth, can be validated and challenged by the experience of others, but it remains limited to the relationship between subject and object.

The primary difference between material, conceptual, and theological truth is their reference points. Material truth refers to the truth of physical reality. Therefore, the reference point (the object in question) is available to the senses. Though we are having a subjective experience of the agreed upon object, it is readily available to be scrutinized. The object of conceptual truth is the concept itself. In this case the object in question (the concept) is in reference to a common experience among humans. Though we may disagree on its nature, beauty is universal to the human condition.

The object of theological truth is not a material object, nor is it isolated to a concept regarding human experience. Theological truth refers to a transcendent reality. While this reality can be considered an object of human experience, it transcends any quality or concept one could use to represent it. There is no proof that God exists—there cannot be. The truth of God refers to the human experience of God within and beyond our very existence. This creates the paradox of theological concepts. The words, ideas, and images used to describe God are incapable of doing so. The best one can do is agree upon a set of symbols that reference God without describing it.

RELIGIOUS EVOLUTION

The root of religion is the subjective experience of God, and all subjective experiences are influenced by the cultural and historical particulars within which the experiences take place. If truth is rooted in the relationship between subject and object, then truth evolves as the subjects and objects do. Material truth, rooted in the objects of physical awareness, changes as the subject penetrates deeper into the fabric of physical creation. Yet as the subject changes in knowledge and understanding, the object changes as well. The same is true for conceptual truth. Concepts evolve as experiences change, as do the subjects having the experiences.

The object of theological truth does not change, nor can it be penetrated by the senses or the mind. The evolution of theological truth is ongoing due to our inability to grasp the transcendent and its all-pervading presence. Nothing we can think or say about God is accurate. And yet, there are innumerable ways to approach a reality that has no boundaries. God is within and beyond all things. The accuracy of theological truth is in the subject's ability to consciously engage the reality of God through conceptual understanding. Humanity has been doing this since the inception of reflective thought, and its evolution continues.

We are constantly creating God in our image, meaning we understand God through the lens of our own experience. As culture evolves, so do the religious traditions within the culture. Currently, Christianity boasts the largest number of adherents. The present state of Christianity, however, is not what it was 2000 years ago. With each shift in cultural and historical evolution, Christianity shifts as well. This is not to say that Christianity at its core is subject to the changing cultural landscape. The core of Christianity remains the experience of God through the image and likeness of Christ. This icon is the bridge that connects the temporal and eternal. As the temporal changes, so must the bridge. It is the eternal, however, which continues to guide the tradition.

All religious traditions evolve to meet the cultural and historical particulars of the moment. Culture is a historical catalogue of the human experience. And religion, as a subset of culture, is a catalogue of the spiritual experience. The experience drives the tradition as the tradition influences the experience. In the past, religious traditions were influenced by the cultural particulars of a given geographical area. Religions would expand to new territories and adapt themselves to the needs of the community. With each advancement in communication, the rate of change would widen and increase. The more cultural information available to the tradition, the greater the possibility for growth.

HERE AND NOW

The communication revolution has created a monumental flux in the evolution of religion. With massive amounts of information being shared every moment, drastic shifts in perspective are inevitable. Religious adherents of every tradition have been learning about ways of being far beyond their own. Changes in the fabric of religion are nothing new. Any religious tradition that survives does so, not in spite of its ability to evolve, but because of it. The unique circumstance facing the current religious landscape is simply the amount of information available. This is not about a popular Buddhist text making its way through the progressive population of the United States. This is about Buddhism as a whole being available to the masses.

When faced with an influx of new information, religious traditions typically respond in one of two ways. Either they integrate the new information into their beliefs and practices, creating a more expansive way of engaging the divine, or they draw back into themselves seeking to maintain their current methodology.[3] Religions have always reacted in these ways, though the process is most visible in retrospect. The current religious landscape is changing as a whole. The communication revolution has made information readily available to the masses. It is no longer a single

---

3. Most traditions find themselves somewhere in the middle.

tradition moving into uncharted territory. It is religion as a whole converging in cyberspace.

Integration

Whether consciously or unconsciously, the contemporary human mind is taking in vast amounts of new information. The natural reaction to an influx of new information is to absorb and apply. This is how the human being has survived and thrived for thousands of years. We experience, we adapt, and we move on. Part of this adaptation is to integrate useful information while discarding information that is unnecessary or detrimental. Our species has evolved to value knowledge above all else. Thus we have an intrinsic desire to acquire and integrate new data, especially when that data seems vital to our existence.

Contemporary humans have seemingly unlimited access to wisdom. Not only do they live in the midst of wisdom traditions already integrated into the cultural landscape, they have access to the world's wisdom traditions swirling in cybersphere. Religion is a catalogue of the spiritual experience. And it is within the spiritual experience that we find wisdom. When we encounter the divine, we are in direct contact with the source of life. This source imparts a non-conceptual understanding upon us. We cannot comprehend the ground of existence. Yet in relation to the divine we can know all things.[4]

God is within all things, and God recognizes God. Therefore, when human beings encounter wisdom, they are immediately drawn to it. Information is everywhere, and we are generally curious about any new data. Wisdom, however, calls to us—source speaking to source. We may have grown up within a wisdom tradition with a specific understanding of God and creation. But wisdom from other traditions will still speak to us. And if we are open, we will begin to integrate this wisdom into our lives.

---

4. Again, this is not a conceptual knowledge, but a spiritual knowing.

The world is full of individuals who have encountered wisdom from sources beyond their geographical locale. And these individuals are part of communities, religious and non. Therefore, the communities are changing as well—specifically, the religious communities. Religion has always adapted. The rate and expanse of adaptation, however, are shifting. Here in the United States, Buddhist meditation and mindfulness practices have become commonplace. And though these practices are not consciously tied to their religious roots, their religiosity is palpable. All over the world religion is meeting religion, and their collective wisdom is expanding.

Opposition

Not all individuals consider the drastic shift in global culture to be positive. Change is difficult. As new ways of encountering the divine become assimilated into a population, old ways may be discarded. In reality, nothing is ever lost. New traditions are built upon the foundation of old traditions. We never lose who we were in the process of becoming new. The person I am today transcends and includes the person I was yesterday. For better or for worse, the present is a result of the past. There will, however, always be those who seem opposed to change.

Though certainly not alone in its resistance to religious evolution, Christian Fundamentalism occupies a unique position among contemporary religious traditions. Christianity is a religion of orthodoxy. This means that being a Christian is about what you believe over what you practice (orthopraxy). Christianity in its numerous variations maintains a strong emphasis on theology. This is the "right" way of understanding God and its relation to creation. As Christianity has spread through the world, its theology has had to adapt. Though the central tenants remain congruent across space and time, understanding and engaging those tenants have changed drastically.

Modernity has ushered in new ways of understanding creation. The scientific revolution has provided insight into the nature of life and drastically changed what is commonly accepted as material truth. All religious traditions have shifted as a result of new scientific norms. Most have come to emphasize the mystery within and over what can be known by the senses. They have granted the physical sciences leave to explore the depths of the material world, while deepening their resolve to understand how God works in and through creation. Christian Fundamentalism, on the other hand, has pushed back, claiming that God's ineffable word has authority over what can be known through the scientific method.

ONGOING

Cultural expressions change as cultures do, and cultures change as people do. Religion, as a specific subset of culture, is not exempt from these changes. Though the foundation of religion is the human experience of that which does not change, the experience itself is subject to the limited comprehension of the human mind. Religions have always evolved—this is how they stay relevant. The religious traditions thriving today stand upon traditions that have faded into memory. Yet nothing is ever lost. Ancient religiosity lives on in the fabric of its contemporary progeny.

No one can know what is to come of the religious landscape. Yet, if what is to come is the result of what is, then religion will continue to evolve into a singular global movement. Religious evolution is the result of direct experiential contact with outside influences. Contemporary religious traditions are communicating directly with one another on a scale previously unthought of. In the years to come, these traditions will likely have such a broad influence on one another that they will shift in one direction. What will the world religion be—a single mosaic of all the traditions that have come to influence it or a conglomerate of various movements with a single purpose? We will have to wait and see.

The Religious Process

All religions share a common root, which is limitless compassion.

—H.H. The 14ᵀᴴ Dalai Lama

Religious traditions have been evolving since the dawn of self-reflection. From the earliest burial rituals to the divine liturgy of the Orthodox Church, practical spirituality has always been a central component of our daily lives. The myths and rituals of religion are guided by historical and cultural particulars, the practical needs of the community, and, most importantly, the spiritual experiences of those involved. The religious process is a sustained conversation between the one who experiences life through us and those seeking to understand it. The process is not perfect. It does, however, continue.

ONE BECOMES MANY

In the creative act, the singular ground of being divides, becoming the God that knows and the God that is known. This division is the single act that sustains all others. When God-the-subject witnesses God-the-object, God-the-object becomes that which can be known—form. Form begets form, and the one becomes the many. God is expressed in and through what God creates. As expressions of God, we have the capacity to experience the one in all things. We find God in nature, art, music, and each other. You do not have to look far to find the peace, love, and joy of God's being echoing within the creative act. And yet, what is found is often lost.

Many

Creation is a menagerie of forms interacting with one another, and each moment affords us the opportunity to be swept away by the beauty of it all. God is within and beyond the innumerable forms that make up this moment. So, why is it that we fail to recognize the one in the many? If God is fully available to us here and now, how do we miss it? As human expressions of being, we are the many rising from the one and we are the one itself. The physical body, however, is only able to register the existence of other physical forms. And the mind is only able to conceptualize immanent phenomena.

Our physical bodies engage the physical world via the five senses. And the mind organizes these impulses into a picture of the self and creation (subject and object). This is the foundational duality of the human experience—I am the unique entity experiencing the forms surrounding me.[1] It is the mind which organizes and sustains the human person as an individual and creation as the environment wherein the individual moves. Without the mind, we are merely a hierarchy of forms within a larger hierarchy. The individual "I" is an illusion. Yet it is an illusion that we must participate in. The body and mind are forms in a sea of form. However, God is not a form among many. Thus the body and mind are ill-equipped to know God.

All that we can know of life is mediated through our physical experience of it. We gain knowledge through experience and understanding through reflection. This knowledge, however, is limited to the immanent realm. And our understanding is limited to a conceptual framework grounded in the immanent realm. We

---

1. Recall that this duality is a shadow of the primordial duality of God-the-subject experiencing God-the-object.

cannot know an experience that has no definable qualities, and we cannot understand a concept that transcends thought. We are a part of creation, and, as a part of creation, we are bound by the parameters of form. Yet the one is within the many.

One

God is not a form among other forms, nor is God the entirety of all form.[2] God is the formless that gives rise to form. We do not experience God as an object of the senses nor as a thought within the mind. We experience God as *satchitananda*—*sat* (being), *chit* (consciousness), and *ananda* (bliss). God is the formless being within and beyond all things; God is the silent witness of forms rising; and creation, as an expression of God, is blissful. We cannot know God the way we know forms within creation, gross or subtle.[3] God cannot be known; God is the backdrop of knowing.

As we experience creation, we experience the creator. We experience God as the horizon which contains the objects of experience and as the ground of experience itself. God is here and now, closer than breath and thought. Faith can be defined as an orientation toward the experience of God resulting in an existential certainty of God's existence. Faith is not the knowing of an object or the realization of a concept. Faith is a turning towards. We are aware of the experience of God at the level of the experience itself.[4] We can only know God as God knows itself.

FAITH

God knows itself as creation. This is the reason that God creates. Creation is an expression of God knowing God. And, just as we

---

2. Pantheism is the theological view that equates God with creation in its entirety.

3. Gross forms are experienced as physical forms rising on the physical plane while subtle forms include both energetic and thought forms—immanent, yet immeasurable.

4. The Spiritual Plane

are God knowing itself as creation, we have an inherent sense of God's presence. This presence is with us always, just beyond reach. We cannot grasp the experience of God; we cannot comprehend it. We can only turn towards it, and in doing so, strive to live in accordance with it.[5] Faith is the central tenant of all religious traditions. Even traditions with little to no concept of God, such as Theravadan Buddhism, are grounded in the faith experience. Remember, one does not need a personified view of the transcendent in order to live in constant relation to it.

The experience of God does not need to be understood or even acknowledged. In fact, many maintain that the ineffability of God is reason enough to either deny God's existence (atheism) or simply to not bother with it (agnosticism). God's existence cannot be proven nor can it be logically deduced. Theism, atheism, and agnosticism have one thing in common—they are equally inaccurate. Theism, in all its manifestations, posits a God that is, at best, a shadow of the ineffable experience of God. Atheism denies the existence of a transcendent reality because believing in a reality that cannot be measured or understood is absurd. And agnosticism refuses to enter into speculation about the reality of God for the same reason that atheism denies it. Thus we have three dispositions in relation to God's existence, none of which can claim absolute validity based upon their own assertions that God is unknowable.

Faith is not belief in things unseen. Faith is not belief at all. Faith is an acquiescence to the mystery of one's being. The spiritual experience does not lead us to any cognitive conclusions. Faith, instead, leads us to the edge of what is knowable. It is from this edge that we peer into the mystery of God. The religious process is to bring one to this edge, to create the circumstances wherein the spiritual experience is made possible. The myths and rituals of religion are born from the spiritual experience. The world's religious traditions are a storehouse of these experiences. They are

---

5. The Arabic term *Jihad* can be defined as "striving." In the Muslim tradition this is often seen as the struggle to live in accordance with the will of Allah.

not proof of the existence of God. They are simply a catalogue of human experience.

PARADOX

Paradox is at the heart of the religious process. We enter into relationship with a reality that we cannot comprehend. And this relationship grounds and integrates the various complexities of our lived experience. It is through the religious process that we come to witness ourselves as a single strand in the tapestry of creation. We are unique; we are momentary; we are fragile; but we belong to that which is eternally becoming. How is it that an ineffable mystery can have such a powerful effect upon our species? We are homo sapien—thinking person. We have carved out an existence based upon our innate curiosity. It is the mystery that grounds us, that guides us.

Curiosity drives the religious process. We have a deep longing to understand every facet of the lived experience, including the nature of experience itself. Who is the one writing this? Who is the one thinking this? And who is the one beyond sight, sound, and thought? God is the horizon within which all forms rise and fall. And God is the one watching the horizon. We cannot know this horizon, nor can we know the watcher. But we can wonder, and it is this wondering that creates myth and enacts ritual. Religion is not meant to answer a question. Religion is the question.

ON GOING

There is a tension at the heart of the religious endeavor. This tension is created and sustained by the unanswerable question of existence. In the end, we are not meant to know the meaning of life. Life is not a question but an experience. We are, all of us, participants in God's pursuit of self-expression. We are born, we exist, and we die. And, in the meantime, we wonder. We wonder about the myriad ways that forms interact. We wonder about those who existed before us and how we will become better at being human. And we wonder about God, this elusive presence that is within and beyond all things. As long as we wonder, religion goes on.

On Enlightenment
An Epilogue to Religion

Before enlightenment, chop wood, carry water; after enlightenment, chop wood, carry water.

—BUDDHA

MOST RELIGIOUS TRADITIONS POSIT that the attainment of a supreme spiritual state is not only possible but the overarching goal of the religious process. Though the words and ideas vary among these traditions, it is possible to view them as separate commentary on our relationship to a single reality. By examining various terminology referring to the supreme spiritual state, it is my hope that the reader will begin to understand their relationship to each other and to the one reality. The human condition is one and many. Therefore, comparisons are possible and problematic. Per usual, I ask that this commentary be taken as a journey and not a destination.

NIRVANA

The Sanskrit term *nirvana* can be translated as "blown out or extinguished." In Buddhism, the term is used in reference to a flame, where the flame is symbolic for desire. According to the Buddha, human suffering stems from *tanha*—a selfish craving or "thirst" that can never be satisfied. We thirst for pleasure, goodness, and control. But life is impermanent and chaotic. The more we seek to hold on to that which we desire, the more we suffer. Of course, if we do end up acquiring that which we desire, we are disappointed—it either does not fulfill us or does not last.

The Buddha did not speak much about his experience of *nirvana*. He did, however, outline an eightfold path that one could follow in order to end suffering. Once free of desire—once the flame of *tanha* had been extinguished—the individual could live in a state of peace, accepting all that came his or her way without preference or judgment. There would still be thirst, but the individual would not be imprisoned by it. *Nirvana* is the experience of life free of the desire to make life something it "ought" to be. By opening ourselves to the mystery of creation, we find that all is perfectly imperfect.

MOKSHA

Moksha is also a Sanskrit term and can be defined as release from *samsara*, the cycle of rebirth that is the result of *karma*. Samsara can be thought of cosmologically or it can be considered symbolically. Both posit that life and death exist in a constant cycle. We live and we act. Our actions create *karma*—a cosmic energy that influences the next life that we will be born into. If I act benevolently in this life, I will be born into a benevolent existence in the life to come. Subsequently, the way I conduct myself in the next life will have a karmic effect on the one to follow.

If we consider *samara* as a religious symbol, we could view this moment as a single point in an ongoing cycle influenced by karmic energy. Each moment is born, exists, and dies. The moment that I exist in here and now is a result of the previous moment. Likewise, the moment to come will be the result of this one. Thus the cycle of life, death, and rebirth is happening at every level of creation. *Karma* is the energy that fuels this cycle—the causal factor determining what will come from our actions here and now.

It does not take a leap of faith or reason to see the applicability of *samara*. One does not have to be a mystic to understand the nature of causality. Cause and effect seem to be an existential component in how creation moves. There is, however, a deep spiritual significance that is ignored by materialist views of causality. According to the Hindu traditions, our lives are bound by *samsara*. It is the goal of spiritual practice to attain release from the cycle (*moksha*).

In the *Bhagavadgita*, Krishna, the avatar of Vishnu, tells Arjuna that even if he strives to act with wisdom, he will be bound by his desire. Similarly, the Buddha cautions us regarding our attachment to the desired outcome of our actions. In order to free ourselves from this desire, we must learn to act disinterestedly. We are bound by *karma*, not because it is the nature of *karma* to bind, but because it is the nature of the human to bind themselves to outcome-driven actions. Krishna informs Arjuna that the only way to be free from the cycle of *samsara* is to focus solely on his divine presence.

SAMADHI

According to the philosophies of *nirvana* and *moksha*, we do not find peace because of our preoccupation with experiencing life as we want it to be instead of how it is. Once we are released from this desire (*nirvana*) or escape the cycle (*moksha*), we will experience true peace of mind. *Samadhi* refers to the state of perfect mental concentration. When the mind is free from desire and attachment, it becomes absorbed in the moment. Unlike pain, suffering is a mental phenomenon. We suffer because life is not what we "think" it should be. Our thoughts spin recklessly in an effort to assert control. And, as we have discussed, control is an illusion.

Thoughts are not necessarily good or bad; they are mere commentary. Peace does not elude us because we are thinking beings. Peace eludes us because thoughts are given priority over experience. Yet thoughts are merely an object of experience just like sensory and energetic phenomena. When we let go of our need for control, our thoughts are allowed to settle and our minds find peace with what is. We experience, we consider, we grow in understanding, but we do not judge. This is perfect concentration; this is *samadhi*.

THE KINGDOM OF HEAVEN

In the Christian Gospels, Jesus speaks of the Kingdom of Heaven. Like *samsara*, the Kingdom of Heaven is typically viewed either as a literal reality or a mythological image. However, as with any reference to a spiritual mode of being, the truth is both/and. The Kingdom of Heaven is the reality that we come to inhabit if and when we are able to live according to the will of God. In order to understand the nature of this reality, we must first ask what is meant by "the will of God."

There are innumerable factors influencing each and every decision that we make. Some of these factors are conscious, while the vast majority are unconscious. Choice is the illusion of an agent acting in the manner that most suits the needs of the moment. Understanding what these needs are and how to act in accordance with them is central to human growth. But the question remains, can humans find peace on their own? And, if so, how does one act in the manner most conducive to finding it? In this sense, Jesus agrees with Buddha and Krishna.

It is not just that we are inherently self-serving; we simply have no idea what it would take to find fulfillment. The factors that are influencing our actions are far beyond our comprehension, and, even if we could fathom them in their totality, we would not know how to manipulate them to our benefit. Fortunately for us, it is God's will for us to find peace. In fact, peace is the very nature of God's being. Therefore, if we want to experience peace, all we need to do is find God, or perhaps, allow God to find us.

In the Gospel of Thomas, Jesus says, "The kingdom is spread out upon the earth, and people do not see it" (113:4).[1] According

---

1. Meyer, *The Gospel of Thomas*, 25.

to the Gospel, the reality of God surrounds us. In order to experience this reality, we must see creation as the Christ does. Living according to the will of God is living in harmony with the reality of God, for they are one and the same. Only when I am able to let go of what I believe is right for my life, am I able to find true peace and fulfillment. I am an expression of God; therefore, the peace of God is inherent to my lived condition. The Kingdom of Heaven is creation as God sees it. It is the Christ that reminds us that we have the capacity to see it too.

SATORI

Most spiritual practices are just that—practices. The world's wisdom traditions provide tried and true guidance on how one can find peace of mind. There is, however, a paradox in the idea that we should have to strive to be something that we already are. It is as if the mind has created a problem that only exists within the mind. The mystics see through this illusion and invite us to see through it as well. Spiritual practice is meant to put the individual in the proper mind and body space in order to witness what has always been there.

Satori is a Japanese word used in the Zen Buddhist tradition referring to a sudden insight into one's true nature. According to this tradition, individuals cannot be taught what their true nature is. To be "taught" is to come to a mental understanding, and this would be commentary on our true nature and not the nature itself. Thus it is the practice of Zen to place oneself in a position wherein this sudden realization is most likely. We cannot strive to see the world as it is. We can only look. And we cannot strive to discover our innermost selves. We can only be.

The term *Buddha* means "one who is awake." It is not the desire of a Buddhist to create a state of being other than what they already are. Instead, Buddhists removes all obstacles to their awakening. *Satori* is the "ah ha" moment of the individual who has caught a glimpse of life as it is beyond mental conceptions. *Satori* is both immediate and completely ordinary. The Buddha said,

"Before enlightenment, chop wood, carry water; after enlightenment, chop wood, carry water." Life does not change because we find enlightenment; the Kingdom of Heaven is already spread out before us. Once all obstacles are removed, we see life as it has always been—miraculous.

NOTHING GAINED

With each form that spiritual enlightenment takes, or with each term used to describe the one form, we notice that nothing is gained. The world's wisdom traditions teach us that the divine is within and beyond us at all times and in all places. The goal of spiritual practice is to remove any obstacles that may be obstructing our experience of ultimate reality. The mystics remind us that no one can be told what or where God is. And, in truth, no one has to be told. All one has to do is clear away the clutter. Once individuals catch a glimpse of the transcendent, they will understand. Or they will not understand, and in not understanding they will find peace.

Bibliography

Armstrong, Karen. *The Case for God*. New York: Anchor, 2009.
Campbell, Joseph. *The Hero with a Thousand Faces*. Princeton: Princeton University Press, 1972.
"The Gospel of Thomas." In *The Gnostic Gospels of Jesus*, 7–25. Translated by Marvin Meyer. New York: Harper Collins, 2005.
Huxley, Aldous. *The Perennial Philosophy*. New York: Harper Perennial, 2009.
James, Williams. *The Varieties of Religious Experience*. New York: Barnes & Noble Classics, 2004.
Otto, Rudolf. *The Idea of the Holy*. Oxford: Oxford University Press, 1958.
Rahner, Karl. *The Foundations of Christian Faith*. New York: Crossroad, 2006.
Smith, Huston. *The World's Religions*. New York: Harper One, 1991.

www.ingramcontent.com/pod-product-compliance
Lightning Source LLC
Chambersburg PA
CBHW061513040426
42450CB00008B/1591